D0841650

Where Do I Start?

10 PR QUESTIONS AND ANSWERS TO GUIDE SELF-PUBLISHED AUTHORS

Cherrie Woods

Copyright © 2016 by Cherrie Woods

This book may not be reproduced in whole or in part, in any form or by any means electronic or mechanical, including photocopying, recording, or by an information storage and retrieval system without written permission from Cherrie Woods.

WHERE DO I START?
10 PR QUESTIONS AND ANSWERS
TO GUIDE SELF-PUBLISHED AUTHORS

Edited by Michele T. Callaghan, Sonya Vann DeLoach
Cover design by mitchell&sennaar communications, inc.
Printed in the U.S.A.
Woods, Cherrie

ISBN# 978-0-692-57041-8

WARNING – DISCLAIMER
This book is to be used as a general guide only. Practicing all of the PR tools in this book will not guarantee the success of a readers' book as the author has no way of knowing the quality, type or content of individual authors' books. It is written to empower and educate authors on the current tools/information they need to utilize to assist them in promoting their books only up to the printing date. In addition, this book is only one source of information but there is lots of other available material.

Table of Contents

ACKNOWLEDGMENTS

A special thanks to Karen Pope, the first person who told me I could be a PR guru for self-published authors. I also want to give a special thanks to Maxine Bigby-Cunningham, Melanie Hatter, Denny Hunte and Cornelius Harris for their invaluable input. In addition, I thank the authors – emerging and established, self and traditionally published, who contributed their insightful quotes to this book including: Amy Barone, Valerie Beers, Sheri Booker, Bernadine Evaristo, Nadege Fleurimond, Edward Foxworth III, Marita Golden, Bernice L. McFadden, Dolen Perkins-Valdez, Rhonda Welsh and James Wright.

"Writing is a sacred act of love and faith and generosity. We write in order to know and discover what we need to write. Writing, good writing, is supposed to take time, so slow down and enjoy the journey and where it takes you."

– Marita Golden,
Don't Play in the Sun:
One Woman's Journey
Through the Color Complex

FOREWORD

A writer once told me, "No" when I asked her to read in a reading series I curate in New York City. She was shy and said she doesn't do well in front of crowds. Shock doesn't come close to how I felt in that moment. She was a fantastic storyteller, and I assumed she would want to promote her book. Then I wondered how she was getting her book out to readers in the first place. What exactly was her plan? Did she expect to solely rely on the publisher, despite that every publishing house from top to bottom is suffering with smaller marketing budgets by the year? I walked away both confused and sympathetic.

Gone are the days where an author only had to worry about writing the book and letting, hopefully, good fortune take its course. The publishing market has swelled so much that attracting even a handful of readers' interest is a full-time job. It sounds daunting, but it doesn't have to be.

Where Do I Start? 10 PR Questions and Answers to Guide Self-Published Authors is a vital handbook that every writer, both traditional/mainstream and self-published, should adhere to like a doctor's prescription. Today's crowded market forces every writer to build an image that sells. I'm talking about brand, platform, media interviews, and readings. Word-of-mouth will simply not do. When you run out of relatives, friends and coworkers to panhandle your book to, how do you get strangers to care about your work? In this book, PR veteran Cherrie Woods provides step-by-step tips to help writers navigate the world of public relations. You don't need to spend thousands of dollars to get started. Without early preparation and determination, money is wasted.

Most of us run from the phrase *"sell yourself."* The trick is to assess your book for the correct audience, as Woods shows in basic PR practices. She narrows down the skills into simple directions that will help any writer hit the ground running on the right foot.

I first came to know Woods when she approached me for an interview as she was about to launch her self-published poetry collection, *Free to Be Me: Poems on Love, Life and Relationships*. She was persistent (regarding the interview) and followed up on the publication date. It showed me how much she cared about making sure readers would, at the very least, know about her work. She didn't wait for me to invite her to read in my series, and she gave a superb performance in New York. In this book, Woods offers more than a long-standing track record in PR but also the ability to relate as a self-published writer marketing her writing.

Monique Antonette Lewis, founder of At The Inkwell

INTRODUCTION

Why did I write this book?

"Between 600,000 and 1,000,000 books are published every year in the U.S. As many as half are self-published." – Nick Morgan, Forbes.com

The above statement shows how competitive the book market is becoming. In addition, I'm sure by the time you read this guide, the numbers will have increased. This means that, along with the discipline and persistence it takes to complete a book, authors have to consider how to get buyers for your books.

When the author has a publisher, that third party takes the lead on getting PR for their books. However, for self-published authors, one of your biggest challenges is how to do your own PR if you don't have either the expertise or the budget. *Where Do I Start? 10 PR Questions and Answers to Guide Self-Published Authors,* is a quick and easy-to-read handbook that provides you the self-published authors with specific PR knowledge that will help you do most of your own PR or at the very least understand what to expect from the publicist you hire.

I am a 15-year veteran in the communications field. As well as self-publishing a book of poetry and developing a PR workshop for self-published authors, I have done PR for several self-published authors and continue to carry out a successful PR campaign for my poetry book (on a limited budget). In this book, I share my knowledge and insight, so I can help you learn how to maneuver the world of PR and get your books sold.

One of the most important discoveries I have made is that most authors don't want to read long books on the theory and practice of book publicity. You really want to hit the ground running and often do. Unfortunately, most of the running tends to be in the wrong direction with no compass to guide you. My book is that compass.

I have strategically selected ten questions and answers most frequently asked of me by my clients, at my workshops and from callers during a call-in online radio show, where I was the featured PR expert for authors.

Along with all of the important information in this book, I have included authors' quotes about the value of PR at the beginning of each chapter and a notes section at the end of each question. The quotes are from authors at varying points in their careers and from a variety of genres. Some are self-published, some published with small presses and others are veterans in the field. Try to remember their quotes, as they come from voices with experience.

"A well-written piece of writing without the proper public relations strategy is the same as a tree falling in the forest with no one around to hear it."

– Nadege Fleurimond,
Haiti Uncovered

1

Why did you write your book?

It's said there's a book in all of us...but why do you want to write it?

In September 2014, Dr. Michael Ingram, executive director of the D.C. Poetry Project Inc. asked me to be the call-in PR expert on "Power of Poetics," his online radio show for poets and authors in the Washington, D.C., area. I responded with an excited "YES!" It would be a great opportunity to build my brand – Euphoria! I would introduce myself to the show's listeners as a PR expert, poet and self-published author. In the role of a PR expert, I would talk about the value PR provides to people thinking of writing a book and to authors with published books.

One week before the show, Dr. Ingram and I agreed that I would cover six PR questions and answers specific to authors and their books. Following my presentation, he would open up the telephone line for questions from listeners and he would also share questions from the show's Twitter feed.

I insisted that Dr. Ingram and I discuss one "key" question on the show, "Why did authors decide to write their books?" As we discussed my response to that question, Dr. Ingram expressed concern that my answer could discourage potential authors or authors in the process of writing their books.

Before we discuss the "key" question, I want to share why I decided to write my book. My answer is twofold: to teach self-published authors to do their own PR in an efficient manner so that they can be a success in their genre and to continue to build my brand as a PR guru. Knowing why I wanted to write this book got me through days of writer's block, doubts that my book would sell and wondering if self-published authors would find it useful and if it was worth the time and effort.

I believe writing a book requires the same patience and discipline that it takes to run a marathon—which I have done. It was one of the biggest challenges in my life to date, even though it was only a 5K marathon. I prepared for the marathon for about three months. Some of those preparation days were so tiring and even painful, that I began to wonder why I had decided to take on this challenge. For me, doing that 5K marathon was a way to support one of my favorite nonprofits.

This brings us to the "key" question of "Why did you write your book?" Here are the three of the most frequent reasons authors give:

1. **I want to create a source of income.**
   If the main reason for writing your book is to create a source of income for yourself, then I sincerely hope that you understand that you have taken on a serious business venture. I tell my clients most businesses take three to five years to establish themselves and that writing a book to make money definitely qualifies as a business. Depending on your genre, it can take up to three years or more to write your book, and the PR work begins either after the book is done or during the writing of the book. The key to success for this venture is what **you put in will be what you get out.** Whether you plan to self-publish or to find a traditional publisher, you have a lot of work ahead of you. It is wise to register as a business so you can claim some of the expenses that go along with self-publishing a book. From a strictly PR perspective doing your own PR in this millennium is much easier than previously, as the Internet has provided tools and resources that require very little monetary investment.

2. **I have a message to share.**
   Believe it or not, some authors do not want to make money from their books. I know of only one author like that, but I

know there are others. An author may have something to say that is important—be it a technical, religious or spiritual message—and believe that writing a book is the best medium to share their messages. If this is you, there are many resources to sell your book in an e-book format online or in print form. Depending on your topic, you can give away your e-book the most well-known way—through online booksellers like Amazon or Smashwords, but there are other sites that will help you do that. Do an online search to find them. Also, there are numerous venues, including book fairs, flea markets, church events, libraries, used book stores that would welcome free books. You can also offer books at no cost on your website, through your blog or your social media accounts.

3. **I want to establish myself as an authority/brand.**
You have become popular as a speaker, workshop facilitator or some other kind of expert, and you want to strengthen your brand. To do so, you may choose to write a book. Or maybe you want to build a brand so you choose to write a book first to begin to build your brand. For either option, there are key things you need to do to ensure your book will achieve its goal.

   a) **Specialize your book as much as possible.** Ensure your topic has enough of a specific reader base who will purchase your books. For example, this book is specifically for self-published authors, a group of authors that is rapidly increasing in numbers. Several traditionally published authors have shared that they can also use my book as a resource since publishers' marketing budgets are decreasing, and they now have to do much of their own marketing/PR.

   b) **Ensure your targeted readers need the information.** – I know that self-published authors need this information, based on my clients, from questions at workshops and from general questions asked of me online.

c) **Write about your area of expertise.** Don't start from scratch on a new area of expertise because it will show in your writing.

Dr. Ingram was correct. During the call-in show, several poets shared that my above response to the reasons authors write their books caused them to worry that writing a book involved too much work. They weren't sure if it would be worth the effort. Despite the feedback from some of the callers, I still believe that this is an important question for authors to ask themselves.

Notes

Notes

"You've poured your blood, sweat and tears into writing and publishing your novel. Without a good marketing and PR plan to attract an audience and drive sales, all of that labor could go to waste. Don't make that mistake."

– Bernice L. McFadden,
Gathering of Waters

2

What is your book's genre?

Defining your book and your readers

One of the first questions I ask self-published authors is this: "What is the genre of your book?" Your book's genre defines and determines the direction of your PR and marketing efforts. If I could get $20 for authors who don't know the answer to that question, I probably wouldn't be a millionaire—but I would have considerably more money than I do now.

What is the genre of your book? Genre is the type of book that you have written. The overall genre of your book may be fiction (not true), nonfiction (factual) or poetry. However, there are several sub-categories including health and fitness, self-help, science fiction, mystery and suspense, romance, American poetry and poetry anthologies. This is why it is important to know the genre of your book. Your genre will help you determine who your customers will be and help you focus your PR campaign to maximize your opportunities to sell your book. Knowing your genre will also help you select the right reading opportunities, the best media to pursue for interviews and the best collateral to develop for your marketing campaign.

So how do you decide what is the genre(s) of your book? Well again, fiction, nonfiction and poetry are the overarching genres, and there are many, many subcategories. Go to the Amazon.com website, select the books section and review the list of book categories listed in the left margin of the page. This will help you narrow down the genre choices and determine which ones fit your book. Be aware that the list is long and covers genres from business to science fiction to romance and self-help and health to teen and young adult and more. However, this is a great list of the most popular-selling genres. In addition, Literary Agent Rachelle Gardner describes on her website the below six points that will help you determine the genre(s) of your book.

Here is my secret for figuring out what genre to call your novel: Find ten books whose readers will probably also like your book. When you're thinking about the audience for your book, you should be thinking, "My readers are people who love books such as _____, _____, and _____." What are those books? Now, what genre are those books?

That's most likely your genre. The reason is, genres exist for the purpose of helping readers find the books they like. So if you're having trouble identifying your genre, start with your intended audience and work backwards.

When identifying your genre, remember they aren't cut and dried. People won't always agree about which genre a certain book falls into. Just do the best you can to capture your book with a helpful genre description.

It's okay to use two or sometimes even three words for your genre. Historical romance. Paranormal thriller. Medical romantic suspense. Sometimes people embellish a little: women's fiction with romantic elements. That's all fine, as long as you keep it simple.

If an age group is part of your genre, add another descriptor. YA paranormal. YA romance. General YA. Middle grade adventure. Middle grade fantasy.

Here are some examples of fiction genres: fantasy, science fiction, paranormal, mystery, thriller, suspense, literary, historical, women's, Christian, inspirational, horror, romance, western, crime-detective, action-adventure, commercial, or general.

(From Rachelle Gardner: Literary Agent, Editor & Publishing Coach www.rachellegardner.com)

Once you have decided on your book's genre(s), you need to now determine who will read your book so that you can decide on a targeted PR campaign. Ask yourself the following questions, who do you believe will read your book genre? What is their age group? What is their sex? See the table below for some of the stats available online related to specific types of book genres.

TYPES OF BOOKS READ

By Generation, Gender & Preferred Format

These are some of the results of *The Harris Poll* of 2,273 adults surveyed online between July 15 and 20, 2015.

	Total	Generation				Gender		Education			
		Millennials (18-35)	Gen Xers (36-50)	Baby Boomers (51-69)	Matures (70+)	Male	Female	High School or Less	Some College	College Grad	Post Grad
	%	%	%	%	%	%	%	%	%	%	%
Mystery, Thriller and Crime	47	43	38	51	66	37	55	45	49	44	50
History	33	29	32	35	44	46	23	27	34	36	51
Biographies/ Memoirs	31	24	35	34	31	33	29	24	31	32	51
Romance	27	33	22	25	27	7	44	32	30	17	20
Cookbooks/ Food Writing	26	26	31	25	21	18	33	23	32	24	26
Science Fiction	26	32	28	22	17	35	19	25	29	28	22
Fantasy	24	37	25	15	10	23	25	29	24	17	20
Classics/ Literature	23	32	20	20	17	26	21	15	24	34	33
Health and Wellness	22	27	24	16	19	19	24	19	20	32	20
Religion and Spirituality	20	21	22	18	17	16	23	19	22	20	19
Self-help	19	21	26	15	11	16	22	17	21	22	19
True Crime	19	21	20	17	14	15	22	21	23	15	10
Political	13	12	12	15	16	21	8	7	15	18	23
Current Affairs	13	14	16	12	12	19	9	9	14	17	21

	Total	Generation				Gender		Education			
		Millennials (18-35)	Gen Xers (36-50)	Baby Boomers (51-69)	Matures (70+)	Male	Female	High School or Less	Some College	College Grad	Post Grad
	%	%	%	%	%	%	%	%	%	%	%
Graphic Novels	13	21	15	5	4	16	10	13	14	12	9
Business	11	15	14	7	2	17	6	9	8	16	17
Poetry	9	16	6	5	2	6	11	8	11	7	8
Chick-lit	8	9	9	8	3	1	14	5	11	11	8
Westerns	7	7	4	6	13	9	5	6	8	7	5
Other Fiction	30	27	23	35	36	25	33	26	33	28	37
Other Non-Fiction	25	27	24	26	16	28	22	22	28	24	29

Base: Adults who read at least one book in average year / Note: Multiple responses accepted

(Begun in 1963, The Harris Poll is one of the longest running surveys measuring public opinion in the U.S. and is highly regarded throughout the world. The nationally representative polls, conducted primarily online, measure the knowledge, opinions, behaviors and motivations of the general public. New and trended polls on a wide variety of subjects including politics, the economy, healthcare, foreign affairs, science and technology, sports and entertainment, and lifestyles are published weekly.) www.TheHarrisPoll.com

Notes

_____

_____

_____

_____

_____

_____

_____

_____

_____

_____

_____

_____

_____

_____

_____

_____

_____

_____

_____

_____

_____

_____

_____

Notes

Authors have to wear several hats – graphic artist for the cover, writing content for flow and impact and then promoting the book to their target audience, oftentimes before the book is printed!

– Edward Foxworth III,
The Six Routines of Self-Discovery

3

How do you choose the right book cover?

Your book cover is like a store window display

According to Mark Coker, founder of Smashwords, "In addition to promising what a book will deliver, the cover image also promises (or fails to promise) that the author is a professional, and that the book will honor the reader's time."

Unfortunately, book covers are the area where most self-published authors get a C to D grade. This can be detrimental to the success of your book because in the world of authors, its cover will judge your book. I strongly suggest that, if you have any PR budget, spend your money on paying a graphic designer to design your book cover!

Selecting a cover is not just about selecting a nice picture for your book. Your book cover's purpose is to attract buyers. To help you understand what attracts a book buyer, I want you to select three to four books in your book's genre from your personal book collection, your local library, your favorite bookstore or an online bookstore. Look at the book covers of each of the selected books. Think about what you like about the book covers, what you don't like, what could be better, and so on.

Now you should have a better understanding of why your book cover can make all the difference in whether a reader will purchase your book because as you probably learned from your book selections, a quality image, uniform lettering and an overall balanced design is the appeal that can influence a buyer to purchase your book. A good cover also implies quality book contents. I say implies, because I have purchased a few books with high quality, attractive covers that were not well-written. I'm also certain there are also great books with ineffective covers.

If you do decide to invest dollars to hire a graphic designer to create your book cover, you may want to know where or how to find one. Following are some suggestions on how to find one.

- Contact the graphic design department at your local community college or arts university. There are students there who may do your design at no cost as part of their program or at a low cost to build their portfolios.
- Other authors are also a great resource. Attend author festivals, events or conferences and, if you like a particular book cover, ask the author who did the design and get their information.
- Museums/art galleries are also great venues to call and ask for graphic designer referrals.
- Printing/press companies usually have graphic designers on staff or interact with many graphic designers.
- Online portfolio websites like Behance.com also have a generous listing of graphic designers looking for work and their portfolios. You can usually negotiate with them.

If you absolutely cannot afford a graphic designer to design your cover, then a viable option is to use lettering (fonts) as a design element on your cover. Be sure to keep the amount of fonts you use on your cover to a minimum. I suggest two maximum – one for the title and another for your name. Yes, lettering can be exciting and interesting and there are many available fonts and colors.

Two additional points to consider when selecting your book cover:

- In general, images of people of color tend to attract a readership within that demographic group, though that is slowly changing.
- If your book genre is poetry or nonfiction, it is also appropriate to consider landscapes or objects on your cover.

Notes

Notes

"Writing a book is a big undertaking. If no one knows about it...it won't sell. PR is the key that opens the door to sharing your book with readers."

– Dolen Perkins-Valdez,
Balm

4

How do you build an author platform?

Plat·form - a raised level surface on which people or things can stand

An author's platform is what makes you stand out—things that establish you as an author that will influence readers to purchase your book. It is especially important for self-published authors to develop a platform, because most of you are on your own and no one knows who you are or why they should purchase your book. In addition, if you have any interest in working with a literary agent or a publishing company at some point, then having a platform will play an important role in getting their attention. So what is your platform? It is the factors that give you credibility and makes readers pay attention to you.

As a self-published author, so much of what you do is in isolation, and developing your platform is no exception. What are the things you do, or are, that make you stand out? Is it your years of experience, your educational credentials, are you a popular speaker or is it your profession? In addition, how do readers know about you? Do you blog or have a Facebook page? Do you tweet, Instagram, etc.? So to summarize, your platform covers three areas: Who are your readers? How do they know about you? How do they keep up with your books, activities, readings, and other promotions?

In this millennium, social media has become one of the main tools for measuring your platform. Readers, literary agents and potential publishers pay attention to numbers—how many Twitter followers, Facebook friends, Instagram followers, you have, along with whatever new social media has evolved as important since I began writing this book. This is also where it is important to know who your readers are (discussed in chapter 2) because if you are focused on the wrong social media, then your numbers may be low. For example, if your readers are in the 40+ age group, is Instagram a credible platform to discuss? Facebook may be a better option. Numbers here count for literary agents, because they want to tell publishers that you have high numbers on social media because high numbers suggest that your books will sell, that your readings will have attendees and therefore their job will possibly be easier.

On her website www.janefriedman.com, Jane Friedman, a publishing expert with over 15 years expertise in digital media, describes in the below bullet points what agents and editors typically mean by platform.

- **Visibility.** Who knows you? Who is aware of your work? Where does your work regularly appear? How many people see it? How does it spread? Where does it spread? What communities are you a part of? Who do you influence? Where do you make waves?

- **Authority.** What's your credibility? What are your credentials? (This is particularly important for nonfiction writers; it is less important for fiction writers, though it can play a role.)

- **Proven reach.** It's not enough to SAY you have visibility. You have to show where you make an impact and give proof of engagement. This could be quantitative evidence (e.g., size of your e-mail newsletter list, website traffic, blog comments) or qualitative evidence (high-profile reviews, testimonials from A-listers in your genre).

- **Target audience.** You should be visible to the most receptive or appropriate audience for the work you're trying to sell. For instance: If you have visibility, authority, and proven reach to orthodontists, that probably won't be helpful if you're marketing vampire fiction (unless perhaps you're writing about a vampire orthodontist who repairs crooked vampire fangs?)

Notes

Notes

Writers owe it to themselves to make sure their book is visible. The best way to do that is to include marketing and PR in your budget from the very start.

– Sheri Booker,
*Nine Years Under :
Coming of Age in an
Inner-City Funeral Home*

5

What is your brand?

What makes you stand out from the crowd?

Particularly for those of you that reside in the U.S., the word "brand" is a familiar one because brands like Nike, Adidas, Under Armour, Toshiba, Bausch & Lomb, Audi, McDonald's and Burger King spend millions on advertising to market their brands. More recently, you hear more and more about the technological/telecommunications brands like Google, Microsoft, T-Mobile, Verizon and HP. You're probably saying, "What does a brand have to do with self-published authors?" It may not seem like you need a brand, but it does help to make you stand out.

First, you need to understand the difference between genre and brand. The best example I can think of is Stephen King. When you hear Stephen King's name, what comes to mind? I suspect you automatically think of books/movies like *Carrie, The Shining* and *Green Mile*. Stephen King's genre is science fiction, horror and suspense. But what is his brand? Mr. King's brand includes several elements. His most popular books have set storylines that happen on earth not in outer space. In addition, if you look at most of his book covers, you'll notice there's a similarity in their layout. Most have his name on the top of the page in a large-sized font type and some type of mystical or scary image, be it blood, a skull, or another image that causes a fear reaction. The fact that you think about specific things when you hear Stephen King's name supports that he has a brand. When I think of Stephen King, I tend to know what to expect if I read one of his books—pure, unadulterated fear!

Another author that has a great brand is Terry McMillan. McMillan was the first author to take the stories of middle-class African Americans to a mainstream black and white readership. Though she had a traditional publisher for her first book *Mama*, it was mostly through her own publicity efforts that it became a success. By her third book, *Waiting to Exhale*, she was a household name. Readers familiar with McMillan's work know that her books will tell an urban story about African Americans usually through a woman's voice. And, although her stories differ, there is a consistency and style in her writing that extends to the names of her books, *Mama, Disappearing Acts, Waiting to Exhale, A Day Late and a Dollar Short* and *Who Asked You?*

So what are the best ways for you to showcase your brand? For self-published authors, particularly for your first and second books, your book cover design is probably the easiest way to show your brand. It can be as simple as consistently using the same colors as a backdrop on your covers, the same font, same placement of your name, similar images and shape/size of your book. Also, ensure that your editor/proofreader includes your book cover in their services, because if your cover text has any errors, it will instantly affect your credibility.

A clear and consistent brand will separate you from other authors and help establish your credibility and professionalism as an author. In addition, as you write more books, you will develop your writing style and topic/theme selections.

Notes

Notes

"Social media is indispensable to successfully promoting a new book. Experts say the key is to choose two social media resources on which to devote considerable energy and effort."

– Amy Barone,
Kamikaze Dance

6

What type of online presence do you need?

You can't be on all social channels media

"What online presence do I need" is the most frequent question I have encountered in my conversations with authors? My immediate response would be you definitely need to have a website. Your site does not need to be elaborate, just consistent with your brand. Whether that is using the same colors on your book cover, posting the same headshot used on the back or inside of your book and posting your actual book cover on the home page, brand consistency needs to be evident. I always add that you must be on at least one to two social media channels. The key to social media is to utilize the online tools that you are most comfortable with, and to be consistent, whether you post once a week or five times weekly.

Another important element to your website is to ensure your site has lots of white space, high-resolution pictures/images; your book description, your bio, and a headshot are the basics. You can add on from there—whether it is quotes from your book, press clippings, testimonials, or something else. Also keep in mind, there are several kinds of free website building software online, and/or most web designers can build a basic site for $500 or less.

So how do you know which social media channel is best for you book genre? This is when the demographics of your readers will play a role. Who are your readers? Men? Women? Kids? What age group? If your main reader base is women over 40, then Facebook would be a good option. If your readers are teens, then Twitter or Instagram will be better selections. The key here is comfort and regularity. Whichever social media you choose, get comfortable with it and try to post on it at least twice weekly, preferably on the same days each week. Be mindful of the content of your posts. Try not to just post about yourself. Remember this is "social" media so post about other books in your book genre, inspirational quotes, news stories, interesting authors, events, and so on. Also, remember, if you become depressed or angry—vent in your journal not online.

According to Debra Aho Williamson - eMarketer's principal analyst on www.digitalworld.com, "More than half the U.S. population uses social networks regularly, and Facebook continues to lead the market. But pay attention to mobile social networking, where Twitter, Instagram, Pinterest and Tumblr are all significant players. That's where the next phase of growth is happening."

So despite all of the claims that Facebook is outdated, it's clear it is still going strong.

It is also important to remember that social media is not there to grow your fame; it is a tool to support it, so don't rely only on social media to sell your books. Book sales happen because of your readings, bookstore sales, your personal network and media coverage. It is also important to realize that social media goes both ways. You can also build a network by reaching out to other authors, journalists, magazine editors, and others in the field. I use social media to reach out to other authors both in my genre and outside my genre. Through my growing network, I have learned about reading opportunities, writing courses and conferences that I have attended and have been able to do some important networking and grow my exposure as a result. I was even able to connect with an author who later read the manuscript for this book and provided one of my testimonials.

Notes

Notes

"Authors often say they want 'a little PR' for a project without truly understanding the professional expertise needed for a successful campaign. Developing strong objectives, strategies and tactics is a process authors must begin to engage in if they want to get their work in front of more people. It is not easy but it is of paramount importance that authors gain this skill set."

– Rhonda Welsh,
Red Clay Legacy

7

How do you get local media coverage?

Fifteen minutes of fame

I remember a time when no one knew or even cared what authors looked like or what their speaking abilities were, because the medium for authors was writing. However, that idea has disappeared and now authors, particularly self-published authors have to be seen, heard and do quality book readings – a new skill set for many authors.

Getting media coverage is a great way for self-published authors to receive widespread attention, but I do caution you to do a personal analysis of your interview strengths before you reach out to the media. I know some of you believe that all news is good news, but that is not necessarily true for a self-published author.

Many of you believe you need a publicist to get local media coverage. This is not correct. However it is also not an easy process. You must do your research and lots of preparation to be able to get your own media coverage. Be prepared to speak knowledgeably about the media outlet before you make contact—be it print, radio, television or online. You will also need to compile a list of local media for your city/community. You could purchase a media list from a variety of companies who provide that service or go to your local library, which has catalogs with listings; however, the fastest way to compile a media list is doing online searches under specific search categories. See the four searches below that you should conduct online to develop your list.

- Search for a list of local TV network affiliates/radio stations (radio shows with a talk format) in your city. Listen in to or watch their morning shows to help you understand the format of each show and to get comfortable with their interview styles. Most local network affiliates have a local morning show in most cities that are always seeking interviewees.

- University radio stations are usually looking for stories, so again, a quick online search can help you find those stations

- What are the free community papers in your community? As well as an online search, you will usually see those publications as you move around your city. Community newspapers are usually situated in downtown areas in very visible display boxes, and most libraries usually have most of the more popular ones on display

- Online Blogtalk radio shows are plentiful and always looking for interviewees – ask around or look online. They offer good opportunities to practice or develop your interview skills and it's usually easy to get a recording of your interview.

In addition, you must be diligent…and I mean very diligent. You should think of getting interviews as similar to developing a committed relationship with a new person. Articles about relationships share that it takes three to six months to build a relationship and that there needs to be enough compatibility to make a commitment. So, similar to a romantic relationship, give yourself at least three months to get a commitment for an interview. Spend the first two months preparing for interviews and determining what shows, reporters, etc., would be interested in featuring your book.

Do your self-assessment first and work on developing interviewing skills and then reach out to the show's producer, editor or host (whichever is applicable) to seal the deal on an interview. Think of preparing for an interview as similar to a job interview.

Following are key points that will increase the likelihood of your securing an interview with a media outlet.

1. Begin with doing a self-assessment. I call this "get to know the man or woman in the mirror." Not who you'd like to be, but who you are. It's wise to determine your interview skills, refine them and then select the media you believe suits your skill set.

Self-assessment

Are you good at radio interviews? Are you better in studio or as a call-in guest? If you have a great speaking voice, remember there are numerous online radio shows. Are you a master at TV interviews? Do you have the look, demeanor and voice that would do better in print (newspapers, magazines) or blog interviews? You have to be able to assess yourself or have a trusted friend who will tell you the truth. If your voice is not very strong, it might be best to stick with print interviews (newspapers/magazines, etc.) How do you feel about being on television? Have you been on camera before? Television interviews can be tough. Even if most local morning shows' interviews are only two minutes long, two minutes on TV is a long time.

With phone videos, web cams and other software you can videotape and audiotape yourself and self-assess or ask a few friends or colleagues for their input. Be prepared though, it takes a lot of practice!

---

2. Ensure your author "Electronic Toolkit" is ready and adequate. What is your electronic toolkit? It includes your color headshot (300 dpi), color book cover (300 dpi), 150-word bio and 200-word book synopsis (short description of your book's contents – written to garner interest in your book). What is dpi? It means dots per inch, which indicates the quality of your photo. Because a 300 dpi is required if your photo/book cover is used in a print publication, I suggest authors ensure both their headshot and book cover are 300 dpi. How do you check the quality level of your photos? Right click on your photo, go to Properties, and then click on Details and scroll down until you see the letters "dpi." The number in front of those letters is your photos' dpi.

3. Be sure to learn as much as possible about the show, segment, newspaper or magazine. How do you get that knowledge? Watch or listen to the show/segment for at least one month before calling to ask how to get an interview. Read everything about the show and the host(s) online. Pay attention to the host's interview style. Read at least two issues of a monthly publication and at least two weeks of a daily or weekly newspaper.

4. Does the media outlet/publication interview or feature authors?

5. What topics does the show cover and does your book address these topics? How long are the articles in the printed publication or blog?

6. How long are the typical interviews on this show? Radio interviews tend to be at least 20 minutes. TV interviews on morning shows are about two minutes.

7. When does the show air? Look up the show's air time on the network's website.

8. When you call, you want to ask for the producer of the show.

9. If you get the producer's voice mail, have a script prepared (written out) to ask the producer about being a guest on the show. You can also make changes to the below script to craft a pitch letter to send via email; look for sample pitch letters online. (See Sample script on the next page.)

10. Other than emails, phone calls or pitch letters, the most effective method to communicate with media outlets are by writing and sending a press release. Press releases, however, require a specific format and writing style that could be difficult for most self-published authors. I recommend that, like designing your book cover, if you have any budget, to spend it here (cost usually range from $150 to $300). However, there are resources/samples press releases and templates online to assist self-published authors. One site to search is createspace.com.

Sample script

Hi, I'm Cherrie Woods, a Baltimore-based author of a self-help guide called *Where Do I Start? 10 PR Questions and Answers to Guide Self-published Authors.* I really enjoy your show and I believe I would be a great guest in May – National Small Business Month – because my book is for the self-published authors who are the new small businesses. My book offers specific knowledge for these authors who usually have none to little budgets for PR. My book has been out for three months ago and is doing very well on Amazon. My book includes everything authors need to know from, "how to select a book cover" to "how to get local media coverage" to "what type of online presence authors need to have." I can send you a book cover and my bio once I get your email address. I am available for an interview with two day's notice. I am excited about the possibility of being on your show.

Notes

*"My first two books were with very small publish-
ers and I promoted them myself. I carried copies of
my books in my bag to hand out to literary critics
and key literature people. Writers have to be pro-
active, resourceful, business-like and tenacious to
stay in the game."*

– Bernadine Evaristo,
Mr. Loverman

8

How will you market your book?

Ready to sell

After reading the previous chapters in this book, you should be ready to get out there to market your book. Though this chapter focuses on marketing materials and venues to sell your books, authors should know that networking also plays a big role in the success of your book. Attend conferences (search for free one-day conferences), book readings, networking events, professional writing organizations' events, book clubs and book associations meetings, and always have a copy of your book, postcards or your author business cards (your basic marketing materials). You never know whom you could encounter at these events.

So now let's discuss your basic marketing materials and I say "basic" because they are as basic as your bio, synopsis and headshot are to your interactions with media. The basics are a table top or floor sign advertising your book, a 4 X 6 postcard and a standard business card – usually designed by a graphic designer. Online design companies like Vistaprint also do designs for a reasonable cost.

Your sign can include just the book cover and a website address or you can add a few testimonials and a short synopsis. The key is to ensure your sign is not too busy and your book cover is the primary focus. There is one exception to this rule. If your book is primarily to support your brand (the third reason for writing a book in the first chapter), then your headshot or full body shot (depending on the size of your signage) should be included on the sign. In this circumstance, you are as important as your book.

The 4 X 6 postcards are primarily for individuals to take away at vendor events or for mailings to venues that may want to consider you for a reading. These should be of a good quality as everything you do, but good is good enough. Business cards are for people who want to do business (book you for an event, purchase a large number of books or carry your books in their bookstore).

Other marketing materials include promotional giveaways like T-shirts, pins or magnets. Potential buyers like to pick up free items.

Once your basics and giveaways are ready, then it is time to physically get out there and sell your book. There are many nontraditional as well as traditional avenues to sell your book. The following list includes avenues for both fiction and nonfiction books.

- Independent bookstores
- Office supply stores
- Outdoor supply stores
- Health food stores
- Book fairs
- Schools
- Garden supplies stores
- Library book readings
- Partner with an organization that supports themes in your book that will sell your books to raise funds for their organization (they can do a markup and you both share a percentage of the profits).
- Conferences

Last, getting a bookstore to carry a self-published author's books will be dependent on your negotiation skills, how you sell the value of your book, your book's genre and the strength of your platform. Practice your approach, know the value of your book and ensure you have visited the bookstore on several occasions. Bookstores usually ask for about 40% of your book sales, but again you can negotiate with them by being clear about the value of your book to their store.

Notes

Notes

From a presence online to readings at a variety of venues, don't let people forget about you. You want "name recognition."

    – Valerie Beers,
      ... details....selected poems by Valeri Beers

9

Where should you try to get book reading opportunities?

Getting out there

There are many reading opportunities available depending on the genre of your book. Again, it is very important to know the genre of your book. The first step for each author is to understand the type of book you've written. For example, my genre is nonfiction and the subcategory is business and self-help (see chapter 2).

Once you know what genre your book is, see the list below of places to contact. What is the best way to contact these places? If you have easy access to the business or organization, if you are comfortable, visit them in person. Drop by the venue/organization with a postcard that gives a synopsis of your book/contact information and a copy of your book. It gives you great credibility for the programming staff to see your actual book. It is up to you to decide to leave a copy of your book or not. Ask to speak to someone responsible for booking or for their email address/phone number. If they are unavailable, ask for their contact information. Contact the booking person biweekly until you get a response. Be persistent but not annoying; weekly communications could be perceived as too much contact. Also, be clear in your emails. If you are unsure about what to say, refer back to my media sample script in chapter 7.

Here is a list of places to contact to ask whether you can read your book.

- Libraries
- Local book readings, events

- Book clubs
- Book fairs/festivals
- Bookstores (chains and independent)
- Writing organizations' events
- Author conferences
- Church events
- Community events
- Museums
- Radio shows
- Open mics
- Book Club and general conferences
- Poetry events
- Holiday events
- Performing arts organizations
- Family events (reunions, weddings, showers, etc.)

These are all excellent options for you to do readings. Again, your book genre can either limit or broaden your reading opportunities. For example, poetry though the hardest to sell, because it has such a niche market, is also the genre that offers the most reading opportunities. I know this because I have self-published a poetry book and I have had many opportunities to read, and because I am also a spoken word artist, I am comfortable in presenting to an audience. I have read at almost all of the preceding locations on the above list.

Fiction writers also have a wide open market for reading, particularly romance fiction writers. Historical fiction appears to be gradually rising to the top. Nonfiction writers, particularly niche writers (writers who write about a specific topic – like this book for authors) do well in sales but do not have the opportunity to read at as many venues.

It is important for you the author to think about all of these factors when you are selecting or creating a list of venues to contact for reading opportunities.

The ability to do a good reading is particularly important for self-published authors. Booking a reading is great, however doing a good reading is necessary because again it adds to your brand. If you are used to being on stage in your work or personal life, that is a huge plus. However if not, then my advice to you is to follow some of my preparation advice for media interview preparation in chapter 7. Videotaping a reading helps you to identify your strengths and weaknesses. Also selecting the right passages to read adds to the quality of your reading. Ensure that the passages you select from your fiction work have interesting dialogue, are action-oriented and have good descriptions. For a nonfiction book, ensure that what you choose to read is relevant and interesting to your audience.

Also, if you can, try to go to the venue where you will be reading in advance, so you get a sense of the amount of space you have to work with. Make sure to arrive early to ensure the sound, lighting, microphone are in working order and suitable for your reading.

Notes

"For me the key to success for any business is to establish a productive relationship with the public. Public relations (PR) and marketing go hand in hand in selling books and making money. For the most part, self-published authors cannot afford professionals who specialize in PR and marketing."

– James S. Wright,
American Apartheid

10

What type of PR work does a publicist do for self-published authors?

Credibility, Credibility, Credibility

Authors often ask me about the differences in doing PR for a tra-ditionally-published and a self-published author. The biggest dif-ference is the constant challenge of assuring readers, editors, press, bookstores, etc., of **the credibility of you the author and your book**. This challenge plays a larger role when your book is nonfiction or if you wrote your book to establish your brand. The question of cred-ibility affects self-published authors in the following ways:

- Getting reviews by the media
- Getting into bookstores
- Being taken seriously
- Getting people to believe that self-published authors can be good writers

More Prep Work is also a huge factor in working with self-pub-lished authors. In fact, a lot of my PR work with self-published authors would fit under what I call the "construction" and "renovation" catego-ries. I usually begin with an assessment of your books and oftentimes your cover, bios, synopses and even headshots may have to be redone to improve the quality of your overall presentation.

Media training is another skill required by self-published authors. A few of my clients have done online or community-based radio, but very few have interviewed for any mainstream/major media. I discuss with my clients how important it is to know what you are good at or as I call it "Know the person in the mirror." Television isn't for everyone. If you don't do well on your local morning show, it will not necessarily end your writing career; however, it will rob you of a good media clip for your website/FB/Twitter pages and the opportunity to perhaps gain some readers. If the interview is not good, you can still get the clip and study it so that your next interview will be better.

Low budgets are endemic to most self-published authors. Authors will pay a high cost to print their books, but they object to paying even 10% for PR to help increase their sales. I believe the reason is most do not understand the value of PR.

Teaching authors about the book world is usually also a part of my tasks. I encourage authors to join writing organizations, writing critique groups, go to book readings, or even read books. Amazingly, I have learned that many don't think about utilizing these resources and don't know how to use them or find the groups/organization. I gently tell authors to search the Internet or Facebook or to ask at their local library. I learned about my writer's association at my local library, because that was its meeting place, and from that group I was able to meet other professionals who provided me with resources and networking opportunities that helped me produce a quality book.

Here's some guidelines to consider if hiring a publicist

If after reading this book, you decide that you do need to hire a PR professional/publicist, I encourage you to take the time to do some research before choosing one. You can speak to other authors who have hired PR professionals, go to vendor events where you can meet even more authors, attend author conferences (there will usually be a PR professional doing at least one of the workshops) and check online for listings of professionals and for pricing information.

Your next step is to determine how much money you have to spend on PR for your book. To do a short term PR project, a minimum of $2,000 per quarter is reasonable to start your campaign. Over a year, plan a minimum PR budget of $8,000 to $10,000. These figures are for an individual PR professional not a PR agency. In addition, these amounts I am quoting depend on what type of and how much PR you need for your book, so costs could be less or more.

When choosing a PR professional, speak to at least three individuals. Discuss your needs and compare what each individual can do for you and their costs. The savvier you are about what type of PR you need (which you now know from reading this book), the more you can negotiate. The $2,000 budget could cover a longer time frame if you know exactly what you need. Also, only work with PR professionals who offer a free consultation. That will help you determine their business styles, help you learn PR language and allow you to ask questions without making a commitment. Ask for references and check out their websites.

Finally, ask for a quote and payment plan options before making a commitment. I encourage you to take your time to think about the quote, what you're getting for the costs, and if you are ready to maximize the PR, you have agreed to pay for. If reading your book isn't part of the quote, then my question to you is, "How effective can that person be in promoting your book?"

PR is important for your self-published book. Make sure you understand what PR is, what it should do for you and that you are getting the best you can for your money.

Notes

ABOUT THE AUTHOR

First exposed to the world of artists by two siblings who are full time artists, Cherrie Woods obtained her first position in arts and culture at Harbourfront Centre (Canada's innovative not-for-profit arts and culture organization). Woods later moved to Detroit, Mich., to work at the Detroit Institute of Arts. Eight years later, she relocated to Baltimore, Md., to head the first department of marketing and PR at the Reginald F. Lewis Museum.

As well as working in the arts, Woods has always done freelance work with artists, small businesses and nonprofits and since 2010 with a variety of authors. Because she assumed that there were enough books written for authors about PR, she created a "Promoting Your Own Book" workshop. However, she later learned that though there are several PR books for authors, most authors were deterred by their length. Woods decided to write *Where Do I Start? 10 PR Questions and Answers to Guide Self-Published Authors* as a quick read for authors to learn the basics for doing their own PR.

Woods is quickly becoming a PR expert for self-published authors through her workshops, seminars and her writings. She plans to write additional PR guides for other artists and small businesses.

To reach Cherrie Woods, email her at info@eclecticpr.com or visit her website at www.eclecticpr.com.

31758504R00046

Made in the USA
Middletown, DE
13 May 2016